OUR GREAT STATES

WHAT'S GREAT ABOUT
COLORADO?

✸ Mary Meinking

LERNER PUBLICATIONS COMPANY ✸ MINNEAPOLIS

CONTENTS

Copyright © 2015
by Lerner Publishing Group, Inc.

Content Consultant: Barbara Headle, Senior
Instructor, History, University of Colorado–
Colorado Springs

Lerner Publications Company
A division of Lerner Publishing Group, Inc.
241 First Avenue North
Minneapolis, MN 55401 USA

For reading levels and more information, look
up this title at www.lernerbooks.com.

Main body text set in ITC Franklin Gothic Std
Book Condensed 12/15.
Typeface provided by Adobe Systems.

Library of Congress Cataloging-in-Publication
Data

Meinking, Mary.
    What's great about Colorado? / by Mary
Meinking.
        pages cm. — (Our great states)
    Includes index.
    ISBN 978–1–4677–3350–2 (library
binding : alkaline paper)
    ISBN 978–1–4677–4707–3 (eBook)
    1. Colorado—History—Juvenile
literature. I. Title.
F776.3.M45 2015
978.8—dc23   2014008813

Manufactured in the United States of America
1 – PC – 7/15/14

COLORADO Welcomes You!

The geography of Colorado makes it the best outdoor playground in the world! Check out the sand dunes and white-water rivers. Enjoy the beautiful scenery by train or by car. Hike ancestral Pueblo trails at Mesa Verde National Park. Strap on skis or a snowboard, and race down one of the state's many mountains. Soak in hot springs, or mine for gold. There's an activity for everyone to enjoy!

Explore Colorado's mountains and all the places in between! Just turn the page to find out about the CENTENNIAL STATE.

WYOMING

NEBRASKA

INTERMONTANE BASIN

Fort Collins

Colorado River

Platte River

Boulder

Westminster

Arvada

Thornton

Lakewood

Aurora

Centennial

Denver

South Platte River

UTAH

N

Mount Elbert
(14,433 feet/
4,399 m)

Colorado
Springs

GREAT
PLAINS

COLORADO
PLATEAU

Arkansas River

KANSAS

Pueblo

Rio Grande

Great Sand Dunes
National Park
and Preserve

Mesa Verde
National Park

Durango

Miles
0   20   40

0   20   40   60
Kilometers

NEW MEXICO

OKLAHOMA

SNOW SPORTS

> Many people think of skiing when they think of Colorado. It is the top location for skiing in North America. You can visit one of more than twenty ski resorts. Try an easy hill if you're new to the sport. If you're a master skier, you can take on one of the harder ski runs.

Keystone in southwest Denver is a great resort for families. Join the Ski & Ride School for skiing lessons. You may meet Keystone's mascot, Ripperoo the dog. After a full day of skiing, explore the Kidtopia Snowfort. Ride the fort's slides, and climb through its tunnels. Grab a cookie at the ice rink, and head to Ripperoo's Village Parade. You can try nighttime snow tubing at Adventure Point. You'll zip down six tubing lanes under bright lights. You may even see the fireworks show!

There are plenty of other winter sports besides skiing or snowboarding. Try cross-country skiing or snowshoeing on Colorado's many trails. Take a sleigh ride through town. Or lace up your skates and hit the ice rink. Colorado is a winter sports wonderland!

Strap on snowshoes and explore Colorado's powdery trails.

Enjoy a horse-drawn sleigh ride through Keystone.

GREAT SAND DUNES

> Would you guess Colorado has a giant sand beach? See for yourself at Great Sand Dunes National Park and Preserve near Alamosa. Here you'll see the tallest dunes in North America. A large lake dried up thousands of years ago. It left behind a large amount of sand. The wind blew the sand to create dunes. The dunes are 750 feet (229 meters) high and stretch 10 miles (16 kilometers) long.

Try sandboarding or sand sledding. Rent special sandboards or sand sleds at nearby Kristi Mountain Sports. You'll hike to the top of a dune before sliding down the sand.

After sledding, cool off in Medano Creek from mid-May through June. This seasonal creek sits at the base of the dunes. The snow in the mountains melts and flows down and around the Great Sand Dunes. You can swim, float on a tube, or skimboard in the creek. Build sand castles with the wet sand. But be sure to visit early in the summer. By August, the creek disappears into the sand.

After playing on the dunes, cool off in Medano Creek.

Try sandboarding down High Dune. Boarding is best after a rainfall.

WHITE-WATER RAFTING

> One of the most thrilling activities in Colorado is white-water rafting. From May through August, the rivers are deeper from the winter's snowmelt. Sign up for a rafting trip on the Arkansas or Colorado Rivers.

Buena Vista claims to be the white-water capital of Colorado. Book a trip through one of more than sixty rafting companies licensed to run on the Arkansas River. Browns Canyon Rafting Company offers family float trips down the Arkansas River and Clear Creek. Choose a calm ride, and let your guide do all the work. Or if you're looking for more adventure, pick a trip that takes you through white-water rapids. Strap on a helmet and a life jacket, and expect to get wet. Grab an oar, and help move the inflatable boat through the fast currents.

COLORADO'S REGIONS

Colorado is one of the most geographically diverse states. It's divided into four regions. The eastern part of the state is the flat Great Plains. The area meets the Rocky Mountains in the center of the state. This mountain range has fifty-four peaks reaching more than 14,000 feet (4,267 m) high. West of the Rockies is the Colorado Plateau. It has hills, plateaus, and flat-topped mountains called mesas. The smallest region is the Intermontane Basin. This northwest corner of the state is known for its rolling, forested hills and flatland.

Experienced white-water rafters often travel in smaller boats designed for two people.

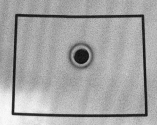

COLORADO GOLD RUSH

> The Colorado Gold Rush happened in the mid-1800s. Miners first found gold in Colorado in 1858. Visit the Country Boy Mine in Breckenridge, and step back in time. This mine produced gold, silver, zinc, and lead. Tour the original mine, and see what it was like to be a miner. Slide down the 55-foot (17 m) ore chute as many times as you want. Spend your afternoon panning for gold in Eureka Creek. If you're lucky, you may find some gold to take home!

In the 1870s, miners found silver in Leadville after the Colorado Gold Rush slowed. The discovery started the Colorado Silver Boom. Leadville soon became the largest silver producer in Colorado. Visit Leadville in August for Boom Days. Grab breakfast, and enjoy some music. Check out the 21-mile (34 km) International Pack Burro Race. Racers do not ride their donkeys. They use a rope to lead them to the finish line!

Stop by the National Mining Hall of Fame and Museum in Leadville. Walk through the Hard Rock Mine exhibit. Learn more about men and women who made a difference in the mining world in the Hall of Fame room.

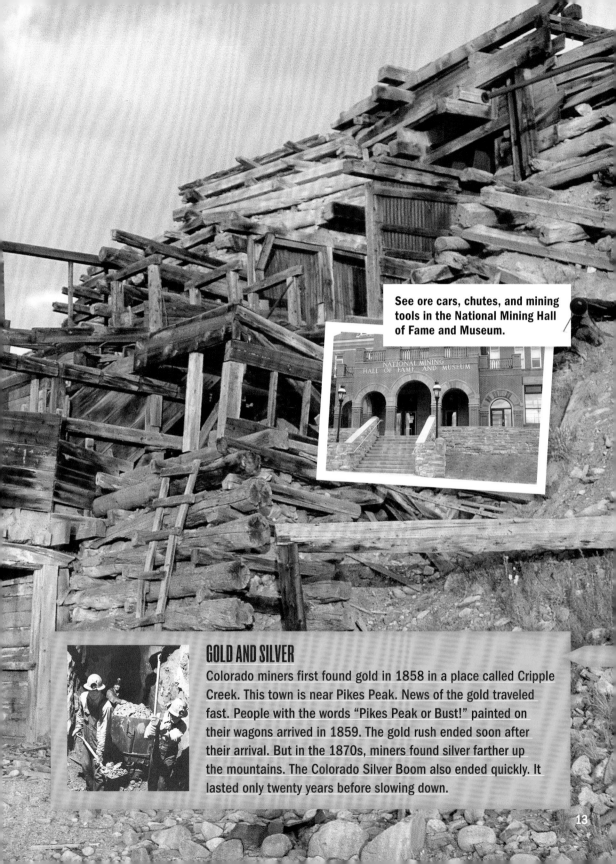

See ore cars, chutes, and mining tools in the National Mining Hall of Fame and Museum.

GOLD AND SILVER

Colorado miners first found gold in 1858 in a place called Cripple Creek. This town is near Pikes Peak. News of the gold traveled fast. People with the words "Pikes Peak or Bust!" painted on their wagons arrived in 1859. The gold rush ended soon after their arrival. But in the 1870s, miners found silver farther up the mountains. The Colorado Silver Boom also ended quickly. It lasted only twenty years before slowing down.

PIKES PEAK
OR BUST RODEO

A young cowboy watches fellow contestants perform at the National Little Britches Rodeo.

> The historic cowboys of the American West influenced Colorado. The western lifestyle lives on through rodeos. Modern cowboys and cowgirls from around the world come to Colorado to compete each year.

Pikes Peak or Bust Rodeo is Colorado's largest outdoor rodeo. It takes place every July in Colorado Springs. Cheer on your favorite cowboys as they compete for a prize. You'll see cowboys riding bareback on broncos and bulls. Make sure to watch the barrel races. Cowgirls race on horses, making three sharp turns around barrels. Try out for the mutton race. You'll need to hold on to the back of a sheep as long as you can. Or you can learn how to ride a pony or pan for gold.

Colorado is home to a rodeo just for kids. More than seven hundred kids ages five to eighteen compete! The National Little Britches Finals Rodeo takes place each July in Pueblo. Enjoy watching flag-racing and rope-tying events.

EARLY COWBOYS

The oldest town in Colorado is San Luis. It is in southern Colorado. Mexican and Spanish settlers founded it in 1851. Mexican cowboys drove their herds of cattle to Colorado to be sold. *Rodeo* means "cattle round up" in Spanish. Today, 21 percent of Colorado's population is Hispanic or Latino.

DURANGO & SILVERTON NARROW GAUGE RAILROAD

> Railroad tracks crossed through Colorado beginning in the 1880s. The trains carried miners and their supplies up the mountains to work. The trains then hauled away the gold, the silver, and the ore the miners uncovered. Take a ride on the Durango & Silverton Narrow Gauge Railroad (D&SNGRR). This steam engine has carried passengers since 1882. You'll travel approximately 45 miles (72 km) between the towns of Durango and Silverton. Grab a snack, and enjoy the beautiful mountain scenery through the windows. If you're visiting during the winter, take a ride on the Polar Express train. Sip hot chocolate as you listen to *The Polar Express* story.

In Durango, visit the D&SNGRR Museum. Look at photographs, paintings, and railroading tools of miners in the 1800s. Check out the telegraph stations and orders that were sent to train conductors.

Explore the insides of
train cars from the 1900s.

Look at photos and books about the
history of the railroad in Colorado.

CITY OF DENVER

> At the heart of Colorado lies its capital, Denver. It's also known as the Mile High City. Even though Denver is at the foot of the Rocky Mountains, it is 5,280 feet (1,609 m) above sea level. That's exactly 1 mile (1.6 km) high!

If you love to spend money, come see where it's made. The United States Mint at Denver makes approximately forty million coins per day. Make reservations before you arrive. Join a free tour to see coins being made, counted, and bagged. Learn more about the original designs of some types of coins.

Spend a day at the Denver Museum of Nature and Science. It is the fourth-largest natural history museum in the United States. See giant dinosaur skeletons and three-thousand-year-old mummies. Grab your hard hat and walk through a silver mine. Learn how minerals form. Dig for dinosaur bones in the Discovery Zone. End your day with a movie in the IMAX Theater or the Planetarium.

Machines at the Denver Mint produce pennies and other coins.

AFRICAN AMERICANS IN COLORADO

After the American Civil War (1861–1865), many African American former slaves moved to Colorado. At the time, as many as one-third of all cowboys were African American. African Americans in early Colorado also worked as miners, soldiers, ranchers, teachers, lawyers, and doctors.

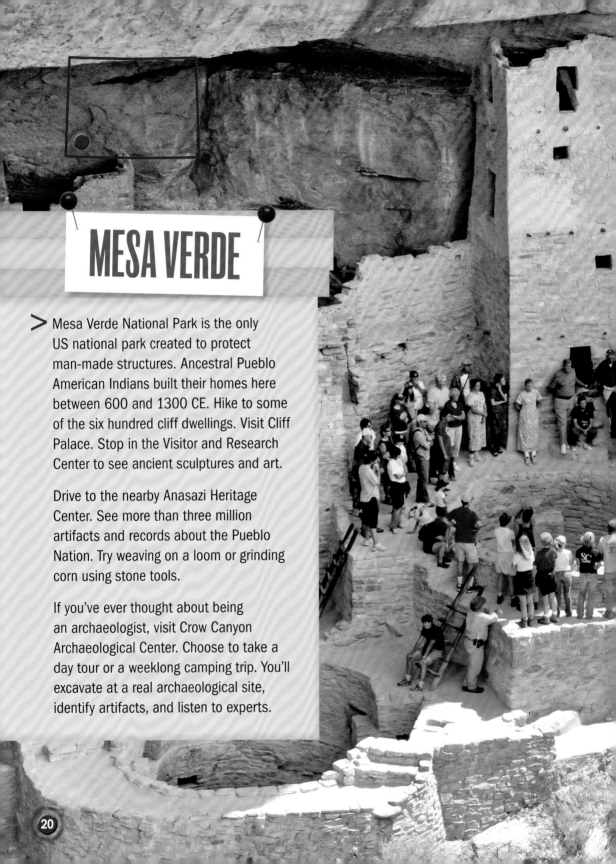

MESA VERDE

> Mesa Verde National Park is the only US national park created to protect man-made structures. Ancestral Pueblo American Indians built their homes here between 600 and 1300 CE. Hike to some of the six hundred cliff dwellings. Visit Cliff Palace. Stop in the Visitor and Research Center to see ancient sculptures and art.

Drive to the nearby Anasazi Heritage Center. See more than three million artifacts and records about the Pueblo Nation. Try weaving on a loom or grinding corn using stone tools.

If you've ever thought about being an archaeologist, visit Crow Canyon Archaeological Center. Choose to take a day tour or a weeklong camping trip. You'll excavate at a real archaeological site, identify artifacts, and listen to experts.

Cliff Palace has 150 rooms and seventy-five open areas.

UTE AMERICAN INDIANS

Around 1630, the Ute Nation began trading with Spaniards for horses. Riding horses helped the Ute hunt and fight for more horses. Approximately 80 percent of land in Colorado belonged to the Ute Nation, but settlers and the US government took much of it. In 1868, the Ute signed a treaty with the government. The treaty gave the Ute people the western one-third of Colorado for their reservation. The Ute reservation is much smaller now. It is 15 miles (24 km) wide by 72 miles (116 km) long. Oil, natural gas, and coal from the land help support the Ute Nation.

21

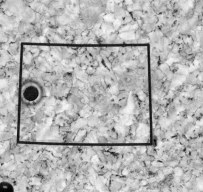

At the Dinosaur Journey Museum, you'll see fossils of many dinos, including a triceratops.

DINOSAUR JOURNEY MUSEUM

> Dinosaurs roamed Colorado approximately 144 million years ago. When they died, sediment covered their bodies, and they became fossilized. Get dirt under your nails at a Dinosaur Dig hosted by the Dinosaur Journey Museum. Dig alongside archaeologists in the desert. You'll help remove large dinosaur bones, log data, and tour the scientists' lab. You may even help uncover a new dinosaur!

After a day of digging, visit the museum in Fruita. Learn about the dinosaurs of western Colorado. See real dinosaur skeletons and modern robotic dinosaurs. Watch scientists studying dinosaur bones in the lab. You can even make your own dinosaur tracks in the sandbox! Uncover dinosaur bones at the Kids' Dig Pit.

Join in a Dinosaur Dig, and you may help find dinosaur bones.

After warming up in the pools at Pagosa Hot Springs, jump in the nearby San Juan River.

HOT SPRINGS

> After a busy trip, you can relax in one of Colorado's hot springs. The world's largest outdoor hot springs pool is at Glenwood Hot Springs. The pool is 90° to 93°F (32° to 34°C) year-round. Jump off the diving board, speed down the two waterslides, or play with your own water toys.

Maybe you'd like to check out Pagosa Hot Springs. The water comes out of the ground at 145°F (63°C). That's too hot to bathe in! The family-friendly springs resort cools the water to different temperatures in its twenty-three heated, outdoor pools. Start in the 114°F (46°C) "Lobster Pot." Then jump directly into the chilly San Juan River. Swim, do laps, or stand under a waterfall. You can even watch trout swim in the river or view movies on the big-screen TV.

YOUR TOP TEN!

You've just read about ten awesome things to see and do in Colorado. Now it's your turn! If you visited Colorado, what would your top ten list include? What places in Colorado do you most look forward to visiting? Grab a sheet of paper and jot down your list. You could even make it into a book with drawings or pictures downloaded from the Internet.

COLORADO BY MAP

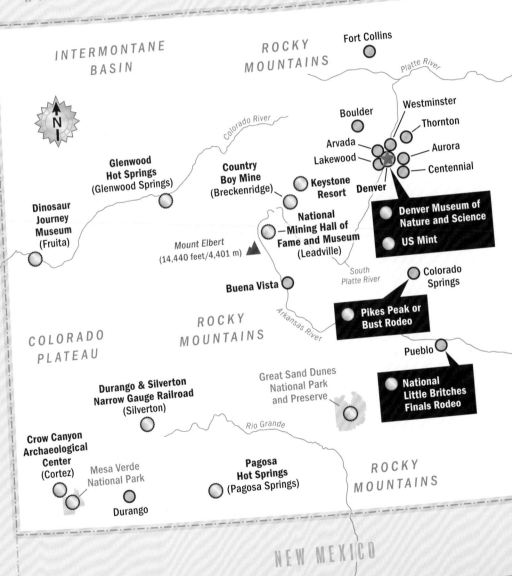

NEBRASKA

WYOMING

INTERMONTANE
BASIN

ROCKY
MOUNTAINS

Fort Collins

Platte River

N

Colorado River

Boulder

Westminster

Thornton

Arvada

Aurora

Lakewood

Centennial

Glenwood
Hot Springs
(Glenwood Springs)

Country
Boy Mine
(Breckenridge)

Keystone
Resort

Denver

Denver Museum of
Nature and Science

Dinosaur
Journey
Museum
(Fruita)

National
Mining Hall of
Fame and Museum
(Leadville)

US Mint

Mount Elbert
(14,440 feet/4,401 m)

South
Platte River

Colorado
Springs

Buena Vista

Arkansas River

Pikes Peak or
Bust Rodeo

COLORADO
PLATEAU

ROCKY
MOUNTAINS

Pueblo

UTAH

Durango & Silverton
Narrow Gauge Railroad
(Silverton)

Great Sand Dunes
National Park
and Preserve

National
Little Britches
Finals Rodeo

Rio Grande

Crow Canyon
Archaeological
Center
(Cortez)

Mesa Verde
National Park

Pagosa
Hot Springs
(Pagosa Springs)

ROCKY
MOUNTAINS

Durango

NEW MEXICO

26

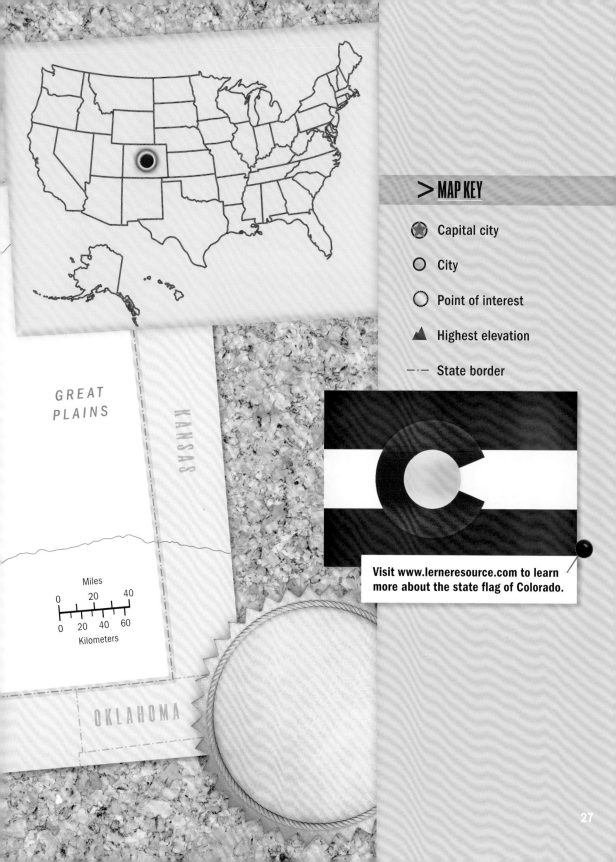

> MAP KEY

⬡ Capital city

◯ City

◯ Point of interest

▲ Highest elevation

–·– State border

GREAT
PLAINS

KANSAS

Miles
0   20   40
0   20 40 60
Kilometers

OKLAHOMA

Visit www.lerneresource.com to learn
more about the state flag of Colorado.

COLORADO FACTS

NICKNAME: the Centennial State

SONG: "Where the Columbines Grow" by A. J. Fynn

MOTTO: *Nil sine numine*, or "Nothing without providence"

> **FLOWER:** Rocky Mountain columbine

TREE: Colorado blue spruce

BIRD: lark bunting

> **ANIMAL:** Rocky Mountain bighorn sheep

DATE AND RANK OF STATEHOOD: August 1, 1876; the 38th state

CAPITAL: Denver

AREA: 104,100 square miles (269,620 sq. km)

AVERAGE JANUARY TEMPERATURE: 24.4°F (−4.2°C)

AVERAGE JULY TEMPERATURE: 68°F (20°C)

POPULATION AND RANK: 5,187,582; 22nd (2012)

MAJOR CITIES AND POPULATIONS: Denver (634,265), Colorado Springs (431,834), Aurora (339,030), Fort Collins (148,612), Lakewood (145,516)

NUMBER OF US CONGRESS MEMBERS: 7 representatives, 2 senators

NUMBER OF ELECTORAL VOTES: 9

> **NATURAL RESOURCES:** coal, gold, natural gas, silver, uranium

> **AGRICULTURAL PRODUCTS:** wheat, hay, corn, beans, sugar beets, peaches

MANUFACTURED GOODS: food, computers, aircraft, machinery

STATE HOLIDAYS AND CELEBRATIONS: Colorado Day

GLOSSARY

archaeologist: a scientist who studies fossils, monuments, and tools left behind by ancient peoples

artifact: a simple object showing human work and representing a culture

bronco: an untamed or partly tamed horse from western North America

chute: a sloping, downward passage

excavate: to uncover by digging away dirt and earth

geography: natural parts of an area

ore: a naturally occurring mineral that contains a valuable substance

plateau: a broad, flat area of land

reservation: an area of public land set aside for special use

resort: a place providing recreation and entertainment to vacationers

sediment: material deposited by water, wind, or glaciers

skimboard: a small surfboard without fins

telegraph: an electric device for sending messages by a code over wires

FURTHER INFORMATION

Bureau of Land Management—Colorado: Activities for Kids
http://www.blm.gov/co/st/en/BLM_Resources/environmental_education
/activities_for_kids.html
Enjoy coloring books, puzzles, and games about fossils, wildflowers, Smokey
Bear, and wild horses.

Frachetti, Suzanne. *Clara Brown: African-American Pioneer.* Palmer Lake, CO:
Filter Press, 2011. Read the story of Clara Brown. She was born a slave, was
granted her freedom, worked her way to Colorado, started a laundry business,
and earned money to free other slaves.

Heos, Bridget. *Colorado: Past and Present*. New York: Rosen Publishing,
2011. Explore the history and places of Colorado in this book.

PBS Kid's Dinosaur Train
http://pbskids.org/dinosaurtrain
Check out this animated site with games, coloring pages, videos, and a
printable dinosaur field guide.

The United States Mint at Denver
http://www.usmint.gov/kids/coinnews/mintfacilities/den
Here you'll find many interactive games, puzzles, fun facts, movies, and the
history of the mint and coins.

Wiatrowski, Claude. *Railroads of Colorado: Your Guide to Colorado's Historic
Trains and Railway Sites*. Helena, MT: Farcountry Press, 2012. Learn about
railroads, railroad towns, history, and maps of railroads in Colorado.

INDEX

PHOTO ACKNOWLEDGMENTS

The images in this book are used with the permission of: © hiramtom/iStockphoto, p. 1; © Andrew Conway/iStockphoto, p. 4; © Jordan McCullough/Thinkstock, p. 5 (top); © Laura Westlund/Independent Picture Service, pp. 5 (bottom), 26–27; © Samot/Shutterstock Images, pp. 6–7; © Steve Estvanik/Shutterstock Images, p. 6; © Bob Winsett KRT/Newscom, p. 7; NPS Photo, pp. 8–9, 9 (left), 9 (right), 20–21; © Ben Blankenburg/Thinkstock, pp. 10–11; © Oleksandr Buzko/Thinkstock, p. 10; © Pacific Northwest Photo/Shutterstock Images, p. 11; © Spirit of America/Shutterstock Images, pp. 12–13; © Andre Jenny Stock Connection Worldwide/Newscom, p. 13 (top); Library of Congress, pp. 13 (LC-USW3-054676-E) (bottom), 21 (LC-DIG-ppmsca-17995) (top); © James Frank/Glow Images, pp. 14–15; © Brian Cahn/ZumaPress/Newscom, p. 14 (top); © Ann Cantelow/Shutterstock Images, p. 14 (bottom); © J. Norman Reid/Shutterstock Images, pp. 16–17; © Russ Bishop Stock Connection Worldwide/Newscom, p. 17 (top), 17 (bottom); © Ambient Ideas/Shutterstock Images, pp. 18–19; © Jim West/Glow Images, p. 18; © North Wind/North Wind Picture Archives, 19; Public Domain, p. 21 (bottom); © Mickey Krakowski/AP Images, pp. 22–23; Ellenm1/Public Domain, p. 22; © Michael Gray/Thinkstock, p. 23; © Pete Mcbride/National Geographic Image Collection/Glow Images, pp. 24–25; ©Melonstone/Dreamstime, p. 24; © nicoolay/iStockphoto, p. 27; © Mraust/Thinkstock, p. 29 (top); © sekernas/Thinkstock, p. 29 (middle top); © Evgeny Bashta/Thinkstock, p. 29 (middle bottom); © zimmytws/Thinkstock, p. 29 (bottom).

Cover: © smithcjb/Getty Images, (Denver Mint); © iStockphoto.com/Suzifoo (mountains); © Josh Schutz/iStock/Thinkstock, (rafting); © Laura Westlund/Independent Picture Service (map); © iStockphoto.com/fpm (seal); © iStockphoto.com/vicm (pushpins); © iStockphoto.com/benz190 (corkboard).